Jane Brocket's CLEVER CONCEPTS

Rainy, Sunny, Blowy, Snowy

What Are SEASONS?

M

Millbrook Press · Minneapolis

We are going to talk about
SEASONS.

A season is a time of year. We can divide each year into four seasons: Spring, summer, fall, and winter.

3

How do we know which season it is? There are many signs. We can look at the weather, the light, and nature.

Let's find out more.

In **spring** the days grow longer and lighter. Leaves and blossoms appear on trees. Plants begin to grow and push their way through the soil.

Baby animals are born.

Spring feels fresh and cool and breezy. There are pale blue skies and fluffy white clouds, showers, and sunshine.

Spring colors are clean and fresh.

Spring is a time to run around and play outside, plant seeds, pick daffodils and tulips,

CALIFORNIAN POPPY
Summer Sorbet

RICH BORDER COLOURS

oson & Morgan

Mr. Fothergill

7648 HARDY ANNUAL

Earth Walker

WATERING IN

POMODORO
RED

Mr. Fothergill's
Sunflower
Vanilla Ice

SUTTONS

and jump in puddles. Splish, splash, splosh!

In **summer** the days are long and sunny. The sky is deep blue. Leaves are emerald green. Gardens are full of bright flowers.

MERCADO MUNIC
DE
ABAS

The sun shines, the air is still, and we can hear insects buzzing. **Summer** feels hot and sunny, warm and shimmery.

It's time for sunglasses and bare feet.

But sometimes dark clouds appear, thunder rumbles, and we run for shelter.

In **summer** we
can play outside
all day long,
go swimming, and
pick strawberries.

We can eat ice cream to keep cool and just take it easy.

In **fall** the days grow shorter. The leaves change color from green to gold, yellow, rust, and orange.

Spiders spin webs, and berries ripen on trees and bushes.

Fiery sunsets match the colors of the leaves.

Fall feels crunchy, crispy, blustery, and blowy. Gusts of wind blow leaves off trees and hats off heads.

We need to wear sweaters
and socks to keep warm.

It's time to carve pumpkins, gather leaves, pick crisp apples and juicy plums,

harvest crops, and plant
bulbs for next spring.

23

In **winter** the days are short and the nights are long. Skies are gray and dull or pale and watery.

The trees are bare
and spindly.

Winter feels cold and frosty.
The air is nippy, and the
wind is biting.

It may be snowy and icy
or dry and clear.

Trees and plants stop growing in **winter**. It's time to wrap up in thick coats and watch the sun rise in a silvery sky.

Or stay indoors and keep warm and cozy under blankets with a mug of hot cocoa.

Can you describe the
SEASONS
where you live?

Which season do you like best?
Or do you like them all?

Millbrook Press
A division of Lerner Publishing Group, Inc.
241 First Avenue North
Minneapolis, MN 55401 USA

For reading levels and more information, look up this title at www.lernerbooks.com.

Main body text set in Chaloops Regular 24/32.
Typeface provided by Chank.

Library of Congress Cataloging-in-Publication Data

Brocket, Jane.
    Rainy, sunny, blowy, snowy: What are seasons? / text and photographs by Jane Brocket.
        pages   cm — (Jane Brocket's clever concepts)
    ISBN 978—1—4677—0231—7 (lib. bdg. : alk. paper)
    ISBN 978—1—4677—4761—5 (eBook)
    1. Seasons—Juvenile literature. I. Title. II. Series: Brocket, Jane. Jane Brocket's clever concepts.
    QB637.4.B76 2015
    508.2—dc23   2013044234

Manufactured in the United States of America
1 — DP — 7/15/14

For Phoebe
—J.B.

With many thanks to
Carol Hinz, Anna Cavallo,
and Danielle Carnito